3 Easy Steps
to
Revival

3 Easy Steps to Revival

BY
ADENA HODGES

Circumference Press

3 Easy Steps to Revival

Cover art by Bridgette Millar

Editing and layout by
Circumference Communication
www.CircumferenceCommunication.com

ISBN: 978-0-9789229-6-2

Printed in the United States of America

Dedicated
to
those who are hungry and thirsty
for more of Jesus.

Table of Contents

Foreward

God is unpretentious! He doesn't grandstand or attempt to impress by flaunting His infinite wisdom and supreme power. Though He's the smartest person on any block—more loving than the most caring mother, He does it all, deflecting accolades and despising fanfare.

When God the Son came to Earth in the form of a servant, it wasn't to dazzle onlookers with His humility. He came in obscurity, choosing the lowest position, because that is, in essence, Who He is. He is meek and lowly in heart, pleasantly simple—modest.

These qualities make Him almost unnoticeable—actually invisible. Consequently, His best representatives are like Him: forged in obscurity, created to impress no earthly counterpart, and preserved for the moment a planet is desperate enough to receive their gift.

Because God doesn't seek to amaze, those who are most like Him can be easily overlooked. Adena Hodges is such a person. Unless you draw on her gift, you will miss it. I did for years. She was there, hidden, not waiting to be discovered, but poised, being refined for just the right moment.

This small book will surprise you. In its brevity, you will hear the still small voice of our humble Creator; beckoning "he who is thirsty to come drink," from its profound simplicity.

In its insight, you will see that all revivals begin in one heart, one soul desperate enough to believe in the divine exchange: God's abundance for our lack. But even personal revivals do not come to the unsuspecting, they sweep down from Heaven in response to the deepest longings of an awaiting life. Adena provides keys to empower and revive our hearts and invites us to join her.

Francis Anfuso
Co-Senior Pastor
The Rock of Roseville
March 2013

Introduction

A number of years ago, while still relatively new to the things of the Spirit, I heard of exciting moves of the Spirit, laughing, crying, miracles, etc. referred to as "renewal." When I heard there would be a conference put on by some of the leaders of renewal in our region, I eagerly planned to attend.

My anticipation was high. I believed it would be an experience that would change my life. The meetings were great and I appreciated the teachings. However, while some around me laughed or cried, I felt little, though I was doing everything I knew to "press in."

When it came to the final "ministry time," I had high hopes for some kind of encounter. The leaders asked us to lie down on the floor while they played a video of crashing waves meant to relax us. While I love the ocean, I've felt the power of the big waves. They can be pretty scary. I struggled to find it soothing. Then, someone near me kicked me in the head rather hard.

As if that weren't enough pain, a woman came over to me to minister. She began pushing on my stomach as she prayed something I couldn't understand. Needless to say, I left disappointed. Why hadn't God "touched" me when I was trying so hard to enter into "renewal?"

As I processed this in the days to come, I felt God saying, "I can meet you anytime, anywhere to talk with you. Don't wait for a meeting." I came to see how we can become "addicted" to events or conferences, when God is wanting to encounter us daily in our routine life.

Too often we go to meetings hoping for something to happen that will transform us.

Speakers and writers hope their next sermon or book is going to change the world. There are occasions when something dramatic happens because of an event. But, for the most part, it is the little things, our daily choices, that determine the quality of our life in God.

I don't want to discount the value or impact of conferences or meetings, because God does significantly move in this way. My point is that we can become so enthralled with the meeting "experience" that we miss God in our everyday life.

How do you view revival? Is it about some great conference or event? Historical accounts can lead us to consciously or unconsciously believe it just "happens" at a corporate gathering and then spreads.

If that is the case, you and I have very little responsibility to prepare. We can sit back and wait, watching and hoping the leaders "get it together" or the worship team somehow becomes more anointed.

It reminds me of the Pool of Bethesda in Jesus's day. Day in and day out the sick and afflicted gazed at the water, waiting for the angel to stir it. They believed that whoever entered the pool first would be healed.

There had to have been a dramatic healing at one point for them to believe in this. But they sat day after day waiting and watching, oblivious that the Great Healer, Jesus, walked in their midst.

In the same way, we can be so focused on waiting for the "waters of revival" to stir in our meetings that we miss the Great Revivalist that is among us and in us!

I believe revival begins within us. Yes, there is a real corporate component to revival. However, to avoid the trap of sitting around the pool of Bethesda, I've got to take responsibility. Revival begins with me. How do I prepare myself?

In the following chapters, we will look at

- Three easy steps to position ourselves for revival
- Three transformational prayer models
- Three perspectives that make what is hard become easy

We can't wait for some national leader or ministry out there. Revival starts right here, right now, with you and me. Let's take a break from our "pool watching" and seek the Great Revivalist!

Easy Vs. Hard

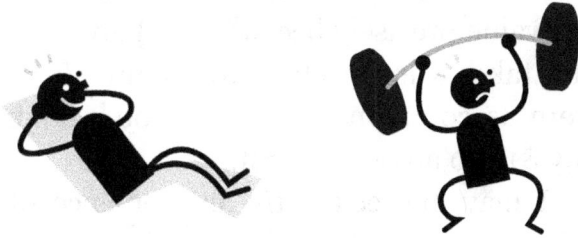

E ver click on those ads to "Lose weight quickly and easily" or "New wonder cure for...?" I confess I have at times fallen to the allure of "easy." It's in our nature to want something quick and painless to work that miracle for us without much effort on our part.

We want that magic pill to drop those 10+lbs or to instantly make us feel better. If the ad read "Most Challenging and Difficult Way to..." we'd hit delete or quickly change the channel.

While we desire the fastest route to success, the reality is that we value those things that are hard to find or difficult to get. Gold has value precisely because it is hard to find and takes a lot of effort to obtain. If gold were as common as granite, you wouldn't pay $1000 an ounce for it.

I may appreciate the convenience of a microwaved meal that is ready in moments, however, I won't value the taste or serve it to my esteemed guests at my next dinner party.

In the same way, if I go to an elegant restaurant and pay $50+ for my meal, I expect to wait while the chef carefully prepares expensive or exotic ingredients for that perfect meal. I'd be insulted if he came back in five minutes with instant macaroni and cheese.

Take lottery winners: A Pentecostal preacher, Billy Harnell, thought his prayers were answered when he won a 31 million dollar jackpot in 1997. Giving up his job as a stock boy at Home Depot, he bought a ranch, six other homes for family members and a number of cars. Life was good for a while; however, like many lottery winners, he couldn't resist those asking for a handout. His life turned sour as he went through a divorce and 20 months after winning the lottery ended up committing suicide.

Unfortunately, Billy's story, or something similar, happens often to lottery winners. Because they didn't have to work hard for the money, they didn't value it or know how to wisely steward the fortune. Some simply gamble it away or use it to get further in debt as they add "must have" luxury items or dream vacations. For others, relationships splinter as greed takes over and divorce, bankruptcy and poverty often follow.

The English proverb "Easy come, easy go" captures this idea that what I didn't put much effort into, I won't value and it will soon be gone – spent, squandered or sacrificed to the gods of this age.

Conversely, those things which cost me "blood, sweat and tears" I will treasure. The teenager who labors long hours to buy his own car will value it more and take better care of it than the one given casually by wealthy parents.

Having said all that, why would I title this book "Three Easy Steps to Revival?" There are paradigm shifts or perspectives that make what is hard, become easy to accomplish. We will look at two of them in this chapter and the final one in the last chapter.

Love Changes the Equation

"So Jacob served seven years for Rachel, and they seemed but a few days to him because of the love he had for her." Genesis 29:20

Seven years of hard labor, easy? Evidently for Jacob those years flew by seemingly without effort because of his great love for Rachel. In fact, because of Laban's deceit, Jacob toiled a total of fourteen years for Rachel. How many young men would be willing to do that today? But for Jacob it was a light thing in comparison to the love and high value he placed on her.

Childbirth is called labor because it most certainly is, yet when you hold that precious bundle in your arms, it feels like a very small thing in comparison.

There is nothing too big or too difficult that parents won't do to save their child, even putting their own lives at risk because of love. A dad running into a burning building to rescue his little one would say he hardly felt the flames and would consider resulting scars nothing compared to the life of his child. He wouldn't be standing there saying, "Hmmm, that looks pretty hard. I don't know if it is worth it."

Wise King Solomon wrote **"...If a man would give for love all the wealth of his house, it would be utterly despised." Song of Solomon 8:7** You can't put a price tag on love, either in labor or money.

Where there is genuine love, that which naturally seems hard becomes easy.

Winner takes all

Reward is another perspective that changes the equation. Athletes train hard for years to compete in the Olympics, often going through painful injuries requiring surgery and lengthy physical therapy. However, those few who stand on the podium to receive a gold medal aren't complaining!

You won't hear them talking about how they wished they hadn't spent so much time training or bemoaning injuries along the way. The reward far outweighs the challenges they faced to get there. To them, in light of the incredible reward and world-wide recognition, their preparation was a light thing.

Or what if you were given a difficult job to do for ten years, but promised at the end of that time that you would receive 100 million dollars. Would it be worth it? Would you spend the whole time complaining about how hard it was or would you be dreaming about how you would use that money in the end? Reward changes perspective.

God combines both of these, love and reward, to offer us incredible perspective on the challenges we face in the Christian walk. If we can view it through those eyes, oh, it IS an easy thing!

This is why Paul could say **"For our light affliction which is but for a moment is working for us a far more exceeding and eternal weight of glory." 2 Corinthians 4:17**

We might say "What? Paul, you experienced beatings, imprisonments, shipwrecks and were nearly stoned to death! You call that a "light affliction?" But he had a grasp of the incredible height and width and depth of God's love and had glimpsed the reward promised to those who "run the race" and, from that perspective, it was "easy" in comparison.

This didn't mean that Paul was oblivious to the challenges. Only a few verses before he reported **"We are hard-pressed on every side, yet not crushed; we are perplexed, but not in despair; perse-cuted, but not forsaken, struck down, but not destroyed." 2 Corinthians 4:8**

Paul recognized the "hard things," yet, put on a scale compared with God's love and promised reward, they became "light." He knew "the end of the story" and that it was worth every challenge.

This viewpoint is mirrored in what is called the Stockdale Paradox, named for Ad-miral Jim Stockdale, U.S. a military officer held captive in Vietnam for eight years. Through much torture, near starvation and deplorable conditions, Jim said, "I never doubted not only that I would get out, but also that I would prevail in the end and turn the experience into the defining event of my life, which, in retrospect, I would not trade."

The paradox was that he observed the POWs who didn't make it were actually the most optimistic. They believed they would be released by Christmas, and then when it didn't happen, they thought they would be out by Easter and so on. They ended up dying from a broken heart as their expectations of soon release were not realized.

Stockdale, on the other hand, accepted the reality of his present circumstances, while holding on to total faith in one day gaining his freedom. He didn't fall into despair or a "just survive until I'm released" attitude. He did everything he could to lift morale, developed a tapping code to communicate with other prisoners and even passed on intelligence information hidden in his letters home to his wife.

In the same way, we can acknowledge the challenges and difficulties we face, but when we know "the end of the story" and God's great love for us, we can persevere and even thrive in the midst of trials.

There have been increasing number of reports of Muslims who encounter Jesus in incredible dreams and, through them, come to faith in Christ. One missionary, getting ready to baptize one of them asked, "Are you sure you are willing to take this step? It may mean your family disowning you, losing your job and possibly your life."

This man replied, "You would not ask that question if you had seen the Man with the kind eyes." Was he facing difficulty and challenge? Yes, but in contrast to those "kind eyes," it was nothing.

I love the chorus "If we could only see a vision of the Lord of glory, it would change everything, if we could see Him rightly." Have you seen those "kind eyes" lately? It changes everything!

We often have a mental concept of God's love, but very little heart connect. Maybe when we first come to faith and, occasion-ally when stirred at a meeting, we feel the passion He has for us. But often, over time, our hearts become dull and we lose that "first love." We become conditioned to messages on the cross and take it for granted.

For some, God's love is an impersonal idea. God loves everybody, right? You may miss the connection of how "head over heels" God is in His love for YOU. Moment by moment He delights in you with singing and dancing! (Zephaniah 3:17) There is nothing you can do that can diminish the affection He has for you. It is real!

In addition, God has a great reward He wants to give to you. Many may consider that this is not a very "spiritual," saying, "He is enough, I don't need any other reward." In fact, there is a song whose chorus goes "We don't want blessings, we want You." However, I don't believe this is Scriptural. God is a giver. That is His delight! The Bible is full of references to the rewards He wants to give YOU.

It's a little like, I may spend many hours figuring out the perfect gifts I want to give my children at Christmas, and then spare

no expense to purchase them and beauti-
fully wrap them, because I want to bless and
delight my children. Christmas morning
comes and I'm almost more excited than my
children are for the moment they will open
their gifts I've so carefully and thoughtfully
prepared.

Than my kids come in and say "Oh Mom,
we really don't want the presents, you're all
that we need."   While I might be touched
by the sentiment of their words, I would be
crushed because I wanted so much to give
these gifts to them.

In the same way, our Heavenly Father
can hardly contain Himself with all that He
desires to shower on us.

Many Christians just think about future
rewards as "sitting on a cloud, playing a harp
for all eternity" which doesn't inspire anyone
and isn't even true!

We read **"Eye has not seen, nor
ear heard, Nor have entered into the
heart of man the things which God has
prepared for those who love Him."
(1 Corinthians 2:9)** and may conclude it

is beyond us. However, the next verse says: "But God has revealed them to us through His Spirit..." He does want to give us those glimpses of what He has for us to encourage and motivate us for what is ahead.

I love to read accounts of those who have near-death experiences, where they get a small taste of what Heaven is like, but return to share their stories. The incredible love, joy, and peace they experience are beyond what our human words can adequately describe.

While Heaven is more than amazing, our final destination is the earth made new. In the age to come, we will be partnering with Jesus as He restores the earth to its intended glory. Trust me, it won't be boring! I can't fully comprehend how it will be, but from the glimpses I've seen, I can't wait!

Our present life is simply a short "internship" and then the real living begins. That doesn't mean we just sit back and wait for the "glory days" to come.

What we do now matters as we learn "in the dark" to trust Jesus, to love Him well without fully seeing ("Blessed are those who have not seen and yet believe." John 20:29), and to represent Him rightly to a dying world.

There are also rewards that He gives us now as we walk in obedience to Him. Sometimes they may be material blessings, but the ones I value most are the internal rewards, building unshakable faith and character.

A few years ago, we went through "the summer from hell" where in two months we went through trial after challenge after heartbreak ending in the murder of our nephew and his girlfriend.

Shortly before, the Lord had given me a dream whose interpretation I understood to mean that if I would stand through the trial, He would reward me with a double portion.

Were there times I wanted to give up? To say it was too hard? That I couldn't understand what was happening or why? Yes, but I knew what He had promised me and that He would give the strength to be faithful. I have seen Him work in incredible ways in our lives since then, as well as working such a grace, peace, and foundation of faith in me that I wouldn't trade for anything.

While the steps I will be sharing in the following chapters may be challenging to our natural flesh, I hope they become "easy" in the light of those "kind eyes" and the amazing reward He can't wait to give you!

.

Step One: Die

Raynald III, a 14th century duke in Belgium, had quite the appetite! Recorded in Thomas Costain's history "The Three Edwards," terribly overweight Raynald was captured during a revolt by his younger brother, Edward. Knowing his brother's weakness, Edward constructed a special room around his brother with windows and a near normal size door. Daily he fed his brother delicious food he knew that Raynald couldn't resist. Although all he needed to do to be free was to stop eating so much, lose the weight and walk out of his self-imposed prison, Raynald couldn't do it.

Day by day, year by year, trapped by his appetite, he continued to eat and gain weight. When accused of cruelty, Edward simply replied, "He is not a prisoner. He can leave whenever he wills." After ten years, Edward was killed in battle and Raynald was somehow extricated from the room; however, he died within a year due to his poor health, a prisoner of his desires.

What's holding you back? We've all felt the pull of our flesh in different areas, but if we succumb, the result is the same. Trapped. Hindered. Held captive. A slave. Paul called this our "old man" or the "body of sin" that must be dealt with if we are to walk in the fullness of freedom. **"Knowing this that our old man was crucified with Him, that the body of sin might be done away with, that we should no longer be slaves**

**of sin. For he who has died has been
freed from sin."** Romans 6:6, 7

The first step to position ourselves for revival is to die. Paul said **"...I die daily."** 1
Corinthians 15:31 He was speaking of dying
to our sinful flesh and walking in newness of
life with Jesus.

Many Christians experience plenty of
"resurrection" power - it's just the wrong
kind – the "old man" rising up!

To walk in personal revival, we must first
die to our sin nature, that is opposed to God
and hinders us from walking in the fullness
He has for us. Then we've got to make sure
it isn't coming back up again!

Elisabeth Kubler-Ross, in her book on
death and dying, relates five stages of dealing with death.

1. Denial - "I'm fine. Nothing's wrong."
2. Anger - "Why me? It's not fair."
3. Bargaining - "I'll do anything..."
4. Depression - "I'm so sad, why bother"
5. Acceptance - "It's going to be okay."

Interestingly, we can go through these same stages in facing our need to die to our sin nature. We try to deny our need to die – "Oh, it's not really that big of an issue." Or we might get angry – "After all I do for you, God, you want that, too?" It's easy to slip into bargaining, "If you just let me do this, I will..." or simply numbing out before finally getting to the place of acceptance and surrender.

But there is a faster, easier way! The first four stages - denial, anger, bargaining, and depression - just slow down the process. Striving and struggling don't work either. I can't do it on my own. It's impossible to crucify myself.

However, I can **turn away** from looking at my weakness, my sin, my brokenness and **gaze** on the beauty of Jesus. When I see the great love He has for me, it becomes natural to **simply yield** and let Him deal with my flesh.

Turn and Gaze

As long as I'm staring at my junk, I can't make any real progress. It can be pretty discouraging! All my efforts crumble away. But when my focus is directed to Jesus, I see it all through His eyes. He didn't sweep things under the rug when it comes to our sins, but neither does He rub our noses in it. He tells us who we truly are to Him, so beloved and cherished that He went to the greatest lengths possible to deal with our sin and to give us hope.

When Jesus encountered the woman caught in adultery, He said, **"Neither do I condemn you, go and sin no more." John 8:11** The love in His eyes and the gentleness of His voice transformed her.

Any condemnation I might feel doesn't come from Jesus, but from the enemy of my soul who wants to keep me trapped in the darkness of despair. But when I turn and gaze on Jesus, when I hear His voice of love calling me beautiful, it changes everything.

Sometimes we can fall into the Greek mentality that our soul and body are "bad" and "sinful" while our spirit is good when submitted to God. This isn't Biblical. God created our bodies as His temple (1 Corinthians 6:19) and He came to restore our soul, (Psalm 23:3) not kill it. He loves how He created my body. He didn't make a mistake.

God loves my mind, and the uniqueness of how I think and feel. While it is true that sin has damaged much, He isn't looking to eliminate whom He created me to be, but to transform me into His image. He isn't looking for a robot or even a clone of Himself. God delights in the distinctiveness of who I am. He wants to restore and shine His glory through me.

I was raised in a legalistic church where it was implied that emotions were mostly "bad" and had to be strictly controlled. The mind was superior and through reasoning, and the power of the will, we could reign in our emotions to a "tolerable" level. Years later, when we came into greater freedom in the Spirit, I was surprised when a leader encouraged us to "study the emotions of God." What? God has emotions? Yes! And we are created in His image! This doesn't mean we let loose with them at will, but every emotion was meant for a time and a place and when redeemed, gives us the variety and uniqueness of expression that we share with God.

If I try to "crucify" myself, I will invariably cut off or hack to death much that He sees as redeemable, as we see things differently than God does. Only He, through eyes of love, knows how to "crucify" our sin nature, while transforming and restoring our soul. He is the Master Surgeon who carefully cuts away what must go, while preserving those parts He redeems for His glory.

Also, Jesus knows the right timing to deal with each issue we face in our life. Those things that "bug" us about ourselves on the outside, might not be His first priority. If

I go to the doctor and say, "This ingrown toenail is really annoying me. I want you to deal with it now." But the doctor gently says, "I understand it's bothering you, however, the real problem we need to address is that you have liver cancer and it's rapidly spreading to other organs. We've got to focus on it first." It would be foolish for me to argue, "But I don't see that or feel it. I want my toe fixed first."

In the same way, God knows the right timing to deal with our "stuff." Those things we think urgently need to be taken care of might be masking a deeper problem we don't want to face. But often when He attends to the inner issue, the outer will be dealt with. Our part is simply to turn to Him and to yield to His way and timing.

As I gaze on Jesus, my perspective changes and those things I held so tightly, I am now able to fully yield. I can now say, "Yes, Jesus, have Your way. I surrender."

Yielding becomes easy in the light of love. I can let go of my pride, my selfishness, my ambition, and my rights. They pale to nothing in comparison to His love. Sin loses its grip on me, as temptation's pull is thwarted by the stronger draw of love.

It is true that there is pleasure in sin. No one falls into sin and says, "It was so awful I just had to do it." Victory over sin is not found in striving, trying harder or by the strength of our will power. The only way is to find a truer, higher pleasure. **"In Your presence is fullness of joy; at Your right hand are pleasures forevermore." Psalm 16:11** The more we gaze on Jesus, entering into relationship with Him, we find the antidote to sin as we learn to enjoy Him and find the richest of pleasures which leave no sorrow or shame.

Jesus' eyes of fire convey both the incredible love He has for me as well as His holiness that can't tolerate sin. His affection is not permissive or lax. Often our view of "love" is getting whatever we want or we can

35

excuse our sin by believing we can just ask forgiveness and everything is okay.

However, the longer I gaze on Jesus, I am astonished at the depths of feeling He has for me and it causes me to tremble at His power and glory. This "trembling" is the beginning of wisdom and will give me the incentive to turn from sin when I see His holiness. Don't settle for an occasional glance. Behold the Man with the kind eyes. Yield and find freedom!

Tips for Gazing and Yielding

Adoration prayer is a great place to start gazing. Simply declare who God is, His attributes and characteristics. It isn't a time for asking for things. Use your God given imagination as you picture Jesus in these ways and interacting with you in love. Below are a number of attributes listed alphabetically.

Don't be in a hurry. Start simply by saying, "God, You are able." See Him as bigger than any problem or any sin you face. "You are able to do exceedingly, abundantly above all that I could ask or think." He is smiling down in tenderness on you. Continue meditating on who He is and find your problems shrink. This is also a great way to go to sleep at night as you lay aside every care or concern from the day and exalt Him. Take one attribute to meditate throughout the day or go through the alphabet picking one attribute per letter for a more extended time of gazing.

A -Able – Abundantly Available – Attentive – Approachable – Abba Father – Abounding in Love

B – Beautiful – Bears my Burdens – Binds up the Broken hearted – Bridegroom God – Bread of Life – Beloved One –

C – Covenant keeping God – my Counselor – Confident God – my Comforter - Creator

D – Desire of the nations – My Deliverer – My Defender –

E – Emmanuel (God with us)

– Everlasting Father – Encouraging God – Ever-present God

F – Forgiving God – Faithful One – Father –my Fortress – my Friend

G – Good Shepherd – Gracious God – Glad God –Giver of all good gifts – Generous God – Gentle God

H – my Hope - God who Hears me – Helper God – my Hiding place – God who Heals me – Holy One

I – God of the Impossible – my Inheritance – my Intercessor – God of Increase – my Instructor –Indescribable

J – Jesus - Jealous God – the Just One – Joyful God

K – King of Kings – Kind – Kinsman Redeemer

L – Light of the world –Laughing God – Listening God – Lion of Judah – Lamb of God

M – Mighty God – Mindful of me – Merciful – Mediator – Messiah – my Maker - Majestic

N – Nurturing God – Noble – Never failing – Name above all Names

O – Opener of my eyes – Overcomer – Omnipresent – Omniscient – Only begotten of the Father

P – Prince of Peace – Protector God – Powerful – Perfecter of my faith – my Provider – God of Possibilities – high Priest

Q – Quiets me in His love

R – my Refuge – my Rock – my Redeemer – Refreshing God – Restoring God – Radiant

S – my Stronghold – my Shield – Shows me His ways – Savior – Sends help – Sustainer – Satisfying God – Supplier

T – Teacher – Trustworthy -

– Triumphant – Truthful – Tender Shepherd of my soul

U –Uncreated God – Unfailing – Unchanging God – Unending – Understanding

V – Victorious God – Vindicating God

W – always With me – Watchful God who watches over me – the Way – Wise God – Wonderful – the Word

Y – Yahweh – whose Yoke is easy

Z – Zealous for me

Yielding is a continuous process, not a one time event. Throughout the day, as you turn to Jesus, simply say "yes" to Him. In every situation you face, practice that "yes" to His will and ways.

A number of months ago while I was saying, "yes" to Him, I felt Him say, "I want your 'yes' to be bigger, higher, wider, deeper."

As I pondered this, I saw it as opening up more and more to Him. We can feel that we've given Jesus everything – every part of our hearts, and yet He is saying, "There's more. Yield more." Don't be discouraged by this, simply let go and say "yes" again. It matters to Him! It delights His heart as we yield!

Prayers of Confession

We typically think of confession prayers where we list our sins. While there is great value to repentance as God leads, we want to look at another kind of confession – confessing who we are in Christ.

When the voice of condemnation comes, confess who you truly are. There is power in what we speak out loud. When we hear ourselves say something, it puts it even deeper in our heart than simply reading it. Declare truth and feel those shackles break off!

I am a child of God

"See how great a love the Father has bestowed on us, that we would be called children of God, and such we are." 1 John 3:1 (see also Galatians 4:7)

I am no longer a slave to sin

"It was for freedom that Christ set us free; therefore keep standing firm and do not be subject again to a yoke of slavery." Galatians 5:1

I am alive in Christ

"But God, being rich in mercy, because of His great love with which He loved us, even when we were dead in our transgressions, made us alive together with Christ (by grace you have been saved)." Ephesians 2:5

I am loved and chosen by God

"O brethren, beloved by God we recognize and know that He has selected (chosen) you." 1 Thessalonians 1:4

I am an overcomer

"You are from God, little children, and have overcome them; because greater is He who is in you than he who is in the world." 1 John 4:4 (see also Revelation 12:11)

It takes 21 days to establish a habit. Practice prayers of adoration and confession regularly until it becomes a natural part of your day. Instead of turning to condemnation, turn to Him! The rewards are incredible. What seems hard and nearly impossible (death to our flesh) becomes easy in the gazing.

For more on Proclamation and Confession prayers, check out www.proclamationprayers.com

Step Two: Wrestle

The second step to personal revival is wrestling. Often God takes us into situations that challenge us. He isn't trying to overwhelm or discourage us but to cause us to grow as He seeks to conform us to His will.

Many of us get Step One and Step Two turned around as we try to "wrestle" with our flesh and "kill" what God is trying to do in us. When faced with difficulties, we often want to blame the devil and try to bind him, when it may be part of God's plan to "wrestle" with us on the potter's wheel of our life

as He forms us into a vessel for His glory.

We know well the story of Jacob wrestling with God (Genesis 32:22-30). His part was to just hang on. Jacob wouldn't let go until he received what he knew God had promised him and wanted to give him all along. I can't imagine what it would be like to physically wrestle with God through an entire night – scary, dark, hard, exhausting. But it wasn't about challenging God, but God gently testing Jacob. Was he willing to fight for his promises? Would he persist even in the darkest hour when he feared for his life and his family? Did he really trust God?

On two other occasions, Jacob had been touched by the supernatural. When he was fleeing from his brother after stealing the birthright and inheritance, Jacob saw in a dream angels ascending and descending what appeared to him as a ladder between heaven and earth and he heard the voice of

God promise him the blessing of Abraham and Isaac.

A lesser known event happened to Jacob after he left Laban, shortly before the night of wrestling, where the Scriptures simply say, **"So Jacob went on his way, and the angels of God met him…" Genesis 32:1** Wow! I would love that encounter, wouldn't you?

Yet in both of these angelic visitations and hearing God's audible voice, Jacob hadn't been significantly transformed. I'm sure these experiences encouraged him, however, it wasn't until he wrestled with God that Jacob's name was changed and his destiny set.

We can become so focused on the "cool" encounters that we fail to understand how significant are those challeng-ing seasons when we have to wrestle through issues, when we don't understand and it's hard to hang on. Yet these very things often strengthen us,

shape us and typically are more impactful than some of the "wow" events.

I love the song by Misty Edwards' whose lyrics go, "If we don't quit, we win." Don't quit. Don't give up. Hang on and believe the promises He has for you. Run the race set before you. Jump the hurdles. Climb over every obstacle. It's worth it!

Someone else who struggled through challenges was Job. It's easy for us, because we know the backstory of the conversation between God and Satan, but Job was in the dark. One minute he was at the height of success and health, one of the richest men on earth at the time, when all of a sudden everything was wiped away.

Wracked with pain, inside and out, Job suffered, trying to understand, to figure it out. His wife was no help, encouraging him to curse God and die. But Job hung on. His friends came and were so overcome with his grief, they sat in silence for seven days. When they did speak, it was like salt on an open wound to Job as they suggested there must be some cause for this tragedy and it must be him. But through it all, he wouldn't let go, saying, **"I know that my Redeemer lives ...." Job 19:25**

Then God showed up. The light is turned on and Job saw from a new perspective though his immediate circumstances hadn't changed.

But the story wasn't over. God turned to Job's friends and rebuked them, warning of judgment if they didn't offer sacrifice and ask Job to pray for them. (Job 42:7-9)

Now think about it from Job's perspective. Here are these people who have only added to his suffering, criticizing him when he's at his lowest point. Now they are asking him to pray for them? How easy would that be for you?

But Job was obedient. He prayed for his friends and Scripture records that it was when he prayed for them, God restored to him a double portion. **"And the Lord restored Job's losses when he prayed for his friends. Indeed the Lord gave Job**

twice as much as he had before." Job 42:10 There are blessings when we hang on through the wrestling but there's even more when we obey.

Abraham passed the test. The Bible doesn't record his "wrestling," however, anyone in Abraham's shoes would. After waiting years and years for the promised child, now God asked him to kill him. In the brief account, we simply see Abraham's obedience. Only a reading of Hebrews gives a hint of the wrestling he experienced. **"By faith Abraham, when he was tested, offered up Isaac...concluding that God was able to raise him up, even from the dead..." Hebrews 11:17** Abraham believed in God's goodness even in this severe test. He wrestled. He hung on. He obeyed.

Jesus wrestled. In the Garden of Gethsemane, He sweat drops of blood as he struggled as a human with what was before Him. He hung on and He obeyed. Jesus could have said to the Father, "Hey, My buddy, Peter and I, have been talking and we've got a great thing going here. If we just had a few more years of ministry, we could really impact the world." Or "Crucifixion is pretty brutal, how 'bout we just go with the symbolism of the Passover lamb. Slitting my throat would be much easier and not so messy." No. He faced it. He hung on and He obeyed.

Why? What motivated Jesus to hang on and obey? For the joy set before Him (Hebrews 12: 2). What was that joy? To see you and me redeemed! We are His joy! In the same way, through the wrestling we, too, can persevere with joy. He is our joy. This helps to motivate us to hang on and to obey when all is dark and we don't understand what is happening. Tap into joy. Gaze on His face.

What kind of wrestling are you facing? Tempted to sidestep it? To say "get behind me, Satan?" or are you ready to set your face like flint, knowing the joy to come?

Tips for Wrestling

A number of years ago, going through a very difficult time financially, I stumbled on a prayer model that changed my life. Take a Scripture, read it and then pray these three things:

A – Agree with the Word
R – Revelation – ask for more revelation of what it means
K – Keep the Word – ask how to obey

I felt God prompting me to use this model with verses regarding the poor and God's provision. He would lead me to a text and then I would write it out and then write my agreement of the Word, ask for revelation and how to obey. Like this:

"You, O God, provided from Your goodness for the poor." Psalm 68:10

A – I agree with Your Word that You provide from Your goodness for the poor. You are good, very good. Your resources are unlimited.

R – Lord, I ask for greater revelation of Your goodness and Your provision for us today.

K – Help me to keep Your Word by believing and acting on Your promise to provide out of Your great goodness.

OR

"So I will restore to you the years that the...locust have eaten... You shall eat in plenty and be satisfied and praise the name

of the Lord your God, who has dealt wondrously with you and My people shall never be put to shame." Joel 2:25, 26

A – I agree with You, Lord, that You bring restoration fully and completely. I praise You because of all the wonderful things You do for me. I eat in plenty and I find satisfaction in You alone. I am not ashamed.

R – Lord, I ask for greater personal revelation of You as my Restorer, my abundant Provider who satisfies me completely.

K – Father, please show me how to keep Your Word, to walk in obedience to You, believing in Your restoration and abundant provision.

Before it was over, I had pages and pages of these promises. Day after day, I would pray through them. Believe me, most of the time I did not FEEL at all like the words I was saying. It was hard to agree with His Word when my young daughter said all she wanted for Chrismas that year was some milk so she could have some cereal. Or the times we could not pay rent and wondered if we would be homeless. Or feeling ashamed, standing in line at the food bank. Yet I kept repeating His promises over and over with my agreement, as weak as it felt at times.

In a few months, even though our circumstances had not significantly changed, I felt a shift in me and such an increase in my faith. And yes, He always provided, though not always in the way I would have liked or in my timing. But I learned to trust His faithfulness no matter what.

I now see how God was using that "wrestling" time to transform my mind about who He is as my Provider and to increase my level of faith. I am enjoying the fruit that comes from obedience and persistence and I wouldn't trade that challenging time for anything, as difficult as it was.

Are there new challenges? You bet! But instead of looking at it as a negative thing, I choose to hang on and wrestle because I know the great reward.

What area are you wrestling? Agree with God. Ask for more revelation and obey and watch Him do amazing things as you hang on!

3 Easy Steps to Revival

Adena Hodges

Step Three: Abiding

In Step One, through dying to our sin nature, God is uprooting from our lives those things that hinder His plans and purposes for our lives. In Step Two, He is conforming us into His image in the wrestling process. In Step Three, He begins to plant and build in us through abiding.

The word "abide" is first used five times in Deuteronomy as a reference to a specific location, **"...in the place where the Lord your God chooses to make His name abide." (Deuteronomy 12:11, 14:13, 16:6, 11, 26:2).** Most Old Testament references refer to a specific location to God's abiding presence. However, in the New Testament it switches – we become the place where God wants to abide! **"Abide in Me, and I in you...." John 15:4**

How do we abide in God and He abides in us? Many years ago I heard this illustration and it helped me to "get" it. Picture a river of water (representing God) and an empty Styrofoam cup with a hole in the bottom (we leak!). Place the cup in the river and you have an image of what it means to abide in Him (we are in the water), and He abides in us (water in the cup). When I remove the cup from the water, the water drains out of the bottom of the cup.

The reason I use a Styrofoam cup for this illustration is that our sin nature doesn't naturally want to "abide." Because of this, most of us just float a little on the surface of all that God has for us, content with a little bit of God in us. So how do we go deeper?

As I was pondering this, a thought alighted. The root of the word "glory" signifies a weightiness or heaviness. In the past, I've heard speakers relate God's glory as this weightiness and, honestly, it didn't appeal to me much. Being sensitive, I can feel the "weight" of people around me, and if I'm not careful, I can become overwhelmed by it. The thought of God adding more "weight" just felt like a burden. I like to think of the things of God as light and lifting me up.

However, when thinking about abiding and what could pull us deeper into the place of abiding, this idea of the glory of God being "weighty" began to make sense! It doesn't work for us to push and strive our way to abiding, but as we yield to Him and receive more of His glory, we naturally will "sink" deeper into Him!

Now picture the cup upright and a pitcher of water pouring into and around the cup. This is how I believe we often experience corporate meetings. We might feel God's presence washing over us and it can seem like abiding, but remember the cup has a hole in it. As soon as we leave the meeting and have an argument with our spouse or our kids act up or our boss calls, we feel "empty" again. So we want to get back to the next meeting to get that feeling again and we misunderstand the place of abiding.

Abiding is a moment by moment experience with the Lord wherever I am and whatever I am doing. It isn't dependent on an event or circumstances.

There is a corporate place of abiding, but we experience it when everyone is first abiding individually. This is what the disciples felt in the upper room after 10 days of prayer and Pentecost fell (revival).

So what does abiding look like? Whenever God calls us to do something, He will give us the conditions for it (what it looks like), the consequences of not doing it and the blessings we can receive from it.

Conditions to Abiding

Confess that Jesus is the Son of God -
*1 John 4:15 "Whoever confesses that Jesus
is the Son of God, God abides in him, and he
in God."*

To most of us, this seems pretty
simple. However, consider what this meant
in John's day. Persecution against Christians was at a height. Tradition tells us that
several attempts had been made on John's
life and when they couldn't kill
him, they banished him
to the Island of Pat-
mos. Confessing Jesus
as the Son of God meant rejec-
tion from family and friends,
imprisonment and possibly
death.

How committed are you? It's easy
when we are enjoying the comforts of our
culture, to say, "Oh, yes, I would do that", but
when it really comes down to it, could you?
Abiding means being "all in," not holding

back any part and being willing to face any consequences for the sake of Christ.

The word "confess" was significant in that day because the persecuted Christians were given the choice to confess Caesar as Lord and offer incense on an altar or confess Jesus, which meant death. If they wouldn't confess Caesar, then they were turned over to the torturers who would do everything they could, short of killing them, to dissuade them. They were then given another opportunity to confess Caesar, but if they would not, they were given 10 days until their execution.

The purpose of the 10 days was for them to heal somewhat from the wounds of their torture so they wouldn't look so bad at the public execution and also to give them more time to recant. Jesus urged the believers in Smyrna to be faithful until death so they would receive the crown of life. (Revelation 2:10) Who are you confessing? Does your life show it?

Eat His Flesh/Drink His Blood – *John 6:56 "He who eats My flesh and drinks My blood abides in Me, and I in him."* This is a curious condition. What does this mean? Jesus made this statement in his discourse to a crowd of people including many who were "regulars."

The previous day He had multiplied the loaves and the fishes and fed a multitude. Now they were flocking to Him again hoping for another miracle, another meal. Jesus knew their hearts and challenged them, declaring Himself the Bread from Heaven. As He went on to explain that He came from the Father, many became offended and murmured among themselves.

As Jesus continued explaining to them that they must eat His flesh and drink His blood, they became even more uncomfortable. Many who had been "disciples," regular followers of Jesus, walked away from Him. They couldn't understand what He was talking about.

It was easy when their stomachs were full and miracles abounded, but when He spoke words of truth they weren't willing to hear, they turned away. Are you willing to hear the hard truth? Or are you just in it for the benefits?

What does it mean to eat His flesh and drink His blood? We do this symbolically in the communion service, but it's much more than that.

1. Hungering and thirsting for Him. Job 23:12 says, "I have treasured the words of His mouth more than my necessary food." Is there a deep hunger in my heart like that for God? Or am I more consumed by my agenda, ambition or project? It can be easy to just slip into numbness, going with the flow or preoccupied with the routine of life. Hunger is a gift. I want more!

2. **Nourishment**. Is Jesus what I "feed" on? Am I eager to read His words, to hear His voice? Is it what fills me up? Or do I seek fulfillment in other things? Am I a spiritual "anorexic?" If I depend on a weekly sermon for my "food," I'm definitely starving! Teaching is meant to be just an "appetizer" to encourage us to pursue more during the

week on our own. What is your "spiritual" weight? Need to put on a few more pounds? The Word of God will give you all you need.

3. **Delight and enjoyment.** I love that God created a variety of foods with different tastes and textures for us to enjoy. He didn't just give us a pill with all the nutrients we need. He delights in giving good things for our pleasure. In the same way, His written Word, the Bible, has incredible variety from history to romance, story to exhortation. Then when His Spirit breathes on a passage and opens our eyes, we see deeper meaning, and greater understanding as He opens up puzzles and mysteries. We can read the same passage many times and then suddenly, by His Spirit, we see something new and fresh.

If your devotional life is dull or boring, it isn't His fault. Ask for your eyes to be opened in new ways. There is so much more He desires to delight you with!

4. **Sustain, dependence, support.** If you've ever gone on an extended fast, you understand the importance of food and water.

Is it the same with Jesus? Do you feel "faint" if you go too long without Him? "Eat up!"

Walk as He walked – *1 John 2:6 "He who says he abides in Him ought himself also to walk just as He walked."* What does it mean to walk as Jesus walked? Our first thought might be about Jesus' humility or His suffering, both of which are valid. However, one area we might not be so quick to think about is walking as a child of the King! Jesus was fully man and in His humanity did nothing that we cannot do. He kept in tune with His Father and did what He saw Him do. We are called to walk in the same way. The same authority. The same inheritance as sons and daughters. To see the dead raised. To see the sick restored. To see God's Kingdom m a n i f e s t e d in the earth realm. This is abiding!

How will I know how Jesus walked?

By studying His life. Reading the gospels regularly and observing how He responded to different circumstances will give me clues on how I can respond when faced with the same things. Secondly, I listen to the Spirit as He reveals what the Father is doing and what my part is. I abide as I seek to stay in tune with what the Spirit is saying.

Does not sin – *1 John 3:6 "Whoever abides in Him does not sin. Whoever sins has neither seen Him nor known Him."* Whoa, this is a tough one! However, we know from the context of John's letter that he doesn't mean the one who abides is perfect and without sin. In 1 John 1:8 it tells us, **"If we say that we have no sin, we deceive ourselves and the truth is not in us."**

So what does this mean? I believe as He abides in us and we in Him, He is transforming us, conforming us into His image. As we gaze and yield to Him, the desire for sin lessens and our hearts are for Him. We don't want to sin. We want to please Him.

Love one another – *1 John 4:12 "If we love one another, God abides in us, and His love has been perfected in us."* It can be easy to bandy about the "love" word in Christian circles. We've heard it so much. Of course, we love each other. We have to. Right? But it goes so much deeper than mere words and is bigger than just my circle of friends or family. It simply says "love one another."

Actions speak louder than words. Do you reach out to those around you? What about those who irritate or annoy you? Or those you are okay with as long as they stay on the other side of the church building and you don't have to interact with them?

Let's go even beyond that. What about your "enemy?" Oh, we don't have any of those, right? We love everyone! Actually, we just use different terms. Those who hurt us. Those who rejected us. Those who weren't there when we needed them. So we just walk away with some sugar coated, Christian language, saying, "God's calling me to another church" or "I'm moving on" while burying bitterness, resentment, anger and even hate in our hearts.

There was a man who had deeply wounded my family when I was a child. Though I had gone through much prayer and counseling, I still felt somehow blocked in my heart. I'd

forgiven him over and over and yet couldn't feel the significant breakthrough I desired.

Finally one day in frustration, I cried out to the Lord, "How do you see this man?" Instantly, I begin to see this picture of him and me meeting in heaven. I felt such over-whelming peace, joy and love as I looked at this man. It seemed that we understood one another. I could feel his sorrow for what he had done, and yet without shame or hiding.

In that moment, I saw him in a new way, through Jesus' eyes, and it changed me.

About a year later, as our pastor was encouraging us to pray for our lost loved ones, I felt God prompting me to pray for this man. I knew he had been an unbeliever, but when I saw the picture, I just assumed that he must have gotten saved in the intervening years. But now I realize I have the privilege of praying him into the Kingdom. I believe that vision will be fulfilled and look forward with joy to that time.

It is true that some relationships are too toxic to continue in and that some people aren't "safe." But I believe as we see them through Jesus' eyes, we can pray for them and believe for great things! And the wounds of our heart are healed so that we can abide fully in God.

On my own, I'm incapable of truly loving anyone. Only as I see people through Jesus' eyes will I have the right perspective to see them. Only as His love flows through me, can I fully love others. As He fills me with His love, it will overflow to those around me.

Love isn't a nice option. Jesus said, **"This is My commandment, that you love one another as I have loved you." John 15:12** How did He love us? He gave everything, including His life, for us.

In the same way, He asks us to love others. It seems like an impossible task, but He wouldn't ask us to do something if it wasn't possible by His Spirit. Love one another.

Humility – *John 15:5 "...without Me you can do nothing."* True humility is under-standing who He is and who I am. I am nothing without Him. As I gaze on Jesus, I begin to comprehend who He is as the Cre-ator and Sustainer of the entire universe, that He holds all power and authority and that it's because of Him that I take my next breath. Then consider that He laid all that aside to become a man, to suffer and die a cruel death so that He could redeem me and make me one with Him. Now all my ambi-tion, pride and accomplishments seem as nothing. What amazing love and grace! My heart overflows with gratitude and amazement for this wonderful Man.

I also understand that though I am nothing without Him, with Him I can do all things! Humility isn't thinking of myself as a piece of junk, lowly and worthless. Jesus died for me! This means I'm incredibly precious and valuable in His sight! Jesus walked in great humility but also with great authority, purpose and confidence because He knew who He was. He wants me to walk in this way also.

When I was growing up, we lived on 40 acres in the country with a custom home overlooking a beautiful valley with a river running through it.

Although my dad was a doctor, we lived simply and it never felt like we were "rich." However, one day, a new friend came to visit and upon seeing our house exclaimed, "Adena, you guys are rich!"

Horrified, I replied, "Oh, no, we aren't rich." You see, I'd read the Scripture passage where Jesus said, **"And again I say to you, it is easier for a camel to go**

through the eye of a needle than for a rich man to enter the kingdom of God." Matthew 19:24 I believed if we were rich, we couldn't enter the Kingdom of God, because how could a camel go through the eye of a needle?

As an adult, I learned an intriguing truth about the camel and the eye of a needle. In Jesus' day, the "eye of the needle" was a well understood phrase and it had nothing to do with a sewing needle. In those days, walls surrounded the cities for protection from enemies, bandits and thieves. At night the gates would all be closed and barred and then re-opened in the morning. However, what if a traveler came to the city after dark? Left outside, he would be vulnerable to attack from marauders.

There was one small gate called "the eye of the needle" built so that only one person could go through at a time and a gatekeeper would be present to open up for any "after dark" travelers. Now, if a merchant came after the sun had set with his camel laden down with wares he intended to sell the next day at market, could he and the camel get in? This was the question. Yes, it was possible for the camel to get through the gate, but only after first removing all the bundles and packages and then the camel would have to get down low and creep through the gate on its knees. Possible, but difficult.

The rich young ruler whom Jesus spoke this word about was unwilling to unburden himself from his self-righteousness, his pride and his reliance on his wealth. He couldn't enter in.

In the same way, humility is being willing to remove all my self-righteousness, all that I think is "gain" to me and enter in the narrow gate, trusting completely in Jesus and His righteousness. Paul said it this way, **"...I also count all things loss for the excellence of the knowledge of Christ Jesus my Lord, for whom I have suffered the loss of all things, and count them as rubbish, that I may gain Christ." Philippians 3:8**

Humility isn't a gift of the Spirit or even a fruit of the Spirit. It's a choice we make.

"For whoever exalts himself will be humbled, and he who humbles himself will be exalted." Luke 14:11 Humility is a choice I have to make on a daily basis.

Consequences of NOT Abiding

John 15:6 "If anyone does not abide in Me, he is cast out as a branch and is withered; and they gather them and throw [them] into the fire, and they are burned." Wow! So abiding isn't just a nice thing super spiritual people can do! God expects everyone who claims to be a Christian to abide. It's not for a select few. If we aren't abiding.... well, the verse speaks for itself. I don't want to wither and be cast out! Thankfully, He is patient with our immaturity and delights in us in our growing process of abiding. Let's stay connected!

The Blessings of Abiding

Fruitfulness – *John 15:5 – "He who abides in Me, and I in him, bears much fruit; for without Me you can do nothing."* We were created to be fruitful. It was part of God's command in the beginning – **"Be fruitful and multiply; fill the earth..." Genesis 1:27** We are made in God's image. He is fruitful. He loves to create.

Thankfully, our fruitfulness is based on God's evaluation. I could look at many seasons of my life as pretty barren. The routine of everyday life and caring for a family doesn't look or feel glamorous or exciting or productive to the natural eye. Yet from God's perspective, I can be flourishing.

We hear of missionaries who labored years and years in another country, only to die seemingly with no "fruit?" Yet seeds were planted that produced an incredible harvest after they were gone. I'm grateful God reserves judgment until the end of the age when the fullness of our fruit will be seen or the consequences of our sins revealed, if we turned away from Him. So don't judge your fruitfulness by the moment. Be obedient and trust Him for the harvest.

Pruning – *John 15:2* – *"Every branch that bears fruit He prunes, that it may bear more fruit."* We don't like to think of pruning as part of the blessings of abiding, but it is. Jesus says clearly that the purpose of pruning is so that we can be even more fruitful. This is different than Step One where God is dealing with our sin nature to remove those things that hinder us.

Pruning is particularly difficult because often what He removes seems so wonderful and good and fruitful to us and can be hard to let go of. But we have God's promise that the purpose is even greater fruitfulness. If you are in a season of pruning, take heart, be encouraged and prepare for the harvest to come.

Ask what you desire – *John 15:7 "If you abide in Me, and My words abide in you, you will ask what you desire, and it shall be done for you."* What an incredible promise to those who abide!

Does this mean if I want a new car or house that He is obligated to give it to me? Just memorize some Bible texts and then I get whatever I want? No. The *word* here is from the Greek "Rhema" or the Living Word, meaning it isn't about how much Scripture you memorized (although that is valuable), but how the Living Word is dwelling within you.

Is His voice fresh and alive to you as you read the Bible? Do you sense His Spirit guiding you through your day?

In that place of "oneness," His desires become our desires. It's about advancing His kingdom and conforming me to His image, and if this includes a new car or house, great! But more often, it's the deeper things.

Practical Tips to Abiding

You think your life is tough? A Russian pilgrim, in the mid-19th century was orphaned at age two and then injured by his brother in childhood, causing a permanent handicap.

This same brother later stole all his money and set his house on fire. Barely escaping with their lives, he and his wife lived homeless and in poverty for two years until his wife died. He had every reason to be bitter and resentful, but chose instead to seek the Lord.

Traveling from place to place, the burning desire of this pilgrim was how to "pray without ceasing." He heard many sermons about prayer, but not how to actually be successful in prayer. After many years, he met a wise monk (spiritual director) who taught him the "Jesus prayer."

The "Jesus prayer" dates back to the Desert Fathers of the 4th and 5th centuries and began first as the simple repetition of the name of Jesus. Over time it was expanded to "Lord Jesus Christ, Son of God, have mercy on me, a sinner." It became a simple way to "pray without ceasing."

As you breathe in, verbally or silently say "Lord Jesus Christ, Son of God" as an act of worship. As you breathe out, verbally or silently say "have mercy on me, a sinner" as an acknowledgement of your sin and petition for His mercy. It can be shortened to a simple "Jesus Christ, Son of God, have mercy on me."

In the beginning, the spiritual director asked the pilgrim to repeat this prayer 3,000 times a day. At first, he found this difficult, but soon began to enjoy the rhythm of the prayer. When he reported this to the wise monk, he encouraged the pilgrim to now pray it 6,000 times per day.

This is what he shared about the experience: "And what happened? I grew so used to my prayer that when I stopped for a single moment I felt, so to speak, as though something were missing."

After ten days, he talked with the monk again who asked him to pray it 12,000 times a day. This prayer transformed his life. He no longer had to verbalize the prayer. It seemed to have become a part of him, with every heartbeat and every breath. He said, "The prayer had, so to speak, by its own action passed from my lips to my heart. That is to say, it seemed as though my heart in its ordinary beating began to say the words of the prayer within each beat...I gave up saying the prayer with my lips, I simply listened carefully to what my heart was saying."

He began traveling from place to place sharing with others the joy he had found. The Scriptures came alive to him with new clarity.

Though I don't count my prayers, I've found including this prayer as a regular practice of my day, as I go to sleep, as I wake up and in all the little moments of life, keeps me tuned in to God, keeping that conversation going and in a place of abiding.

There are many ways to commune with God in the place of abiding, but I've found breath prayers a practical way to abide throughout the day. Try these other breath prayers:

"I am my Beloved's and He is mine." Song of Solomon 2:16

Slowly breathe in as you mentally say, "I am my Beloved's" picturing yourself secure in God's loving embrace. Breathe out as you say, "and He is mine."

"The Lord is my Shepherd, I have all I need." Psalm 23:1

Struggling with provision? Stacks of unpaid bills? I love to use this one as I go to sleep at night, particularly if I'm stressed about finances. It gets my mind off my problems and onto Him. Breathe in "The Lord is my Shepherd" as you picture Him as your tender Shepherd holding you. Breathe out "I have all I need" from a place of contentment in Him.

"My times are in His hands."
Psalm 31:15

This is my "stoplight" prayer! Have one of those days where you hit every light yellow or red? Before your blood pressure goes too high, try this breath prayer! Breathe in "My times" as you picture your schedule and agenda. Breathe out "are in His (Your) hands" as you see yourself placing them all in His hands, trusting His timing for your day. Do this several times and when the light turns green, you will feel less stressed both spiritually and physically as the deep breathing benefits your body as well.

"Since God is for me, who can be against me." Romans 8:31

Distressed about someone not agreeing with you? Or offended with you? Tempted to think everyone is against you? Before the enemy takes you too far down that path, breathe in "Since God is for me" as you see the God of Universe standing with you. Breathe out "who can be against me" as you picture those you feel oppose you shrink in size and disappear.

"His yoke is easy, His burden is light." Matthew 11:29

When I'm feeling overwhelmed with work and find myself striving to finish a project, I turn to this prayer. Breathe in "His yoke is easy" as you picture the heavy yoke of your own efforts lift off of you. Breathe out "His burden is light" as you receive the lightness of His yoke.

"Whenever I am afraid I will trust in You." Psalm 56:3

Facing fear of any kind? Fight it with faith as you pray this prayer. Breathe in "Whenever I am afraid" acknowledging what is bothering you. Breathe out "I will trust in You" as you mentally give that situation over to Jesus, trusting the outcome fully to Him.

You can take any Scripture and turn it into a breath prayer and even adapt it to wording that may be easier for you to remember or flows better. Intentionally practice a breath prayer 10-15 minutes a day in the beginning and, as it becomes a habit, your response will more likely be to pray than to worry, strive or fear as you grow in "praying without ceasing."

You can do this on your way to work or taking the kids to school or at night as you fall asleep. Take a few moments right now to breathe in His presence.

Confidence - *1 John 2:28 "And now, little children, abide in Him, that when He appears, we may have confidence and not be ashamed before Him at His coming."*

Growing up in a legalistic church, we were taught we had to watch every thought and every word because if we died suddenly, we might not be "saved" if our last thought or word wasn't holy. It created a life of fear, wondering if we were "ready."

Now while I'm thankful for the freedom of God's love, I do want to be careful in my thoughts, speech, and actions. I can have confidence in His salvation, not my own efforts. He wants us to walk in boldness before Him because of Jesus' life and death and our entering into fellowship with Him. (Hebrews 10:19-23)

Abiding isn't just for a select few, but the privilege of all who name the name of Jesus. Tired of drifting on the surface? Let's go deep!

3 Easy Steps to Revival

Adena Hodges

Third Perspective

Three easy steps and then we've arrived? Not exactly. We often think of completing one step and then going on to the next. However, instead of looking at it as stairsteps or stepping stones, think of dance steps which you repeat over and over.

I'm not a dancer and feel rather clumsy on my feet. A few months ago, my son tried to show me some swing dance moves he was learning. He was quite good at them and seemed to do it easily, but for

me, it was difficult. I'd move my left foot instead of my right or pause when I was to be in motion. However, if I took lessons and practiced daily, it could become much easier.

In the same way, these three steps aren't meant to be completed and then move on, but rather to become a way of life. On a daily basis, we can flow with the Holy Spirit as our "dance" partner - 1-2-3, 1-2-3 - as we move through the steps. What might have been awkward or difficult at first becomes easy as we practice. This is the third perspective that makes what is hard become easy!

Think of a concert pianist whose hands easily glide over the keys with amazing ease, creating beautiful music. From hours and hours of practice, he or she has developed "finger memory" so that without thinking about each move, the hands go where they need to, seemingly without effort.

If you or I tried to play the same score without having lessons or practicing, it would be a disaster. To become successful at almost anything takes regular repetition as we grow in skill.

Dying to our "old man" and wrestling through challenges become easier as we do it regularly. Our spiritual "muscles" are strengthened. When tempted by an old habit, we find it takes less effort to resist as we've developed new habits of focusing on and adoring the Lord. Abiding becomes more natural as we live it out, day by day, not waiting for a meeting to feel God's presence.

As we practice these three steps over and over, we will find ourselves in the right place for revival to come. The 120 in the Upper Room were perfectly positioned for the Holy Spirit to manifest in power on the day of Pentecost. It wasn't a random gathering. Those who were there had gone through much preparation spiritually.

Does that mean they were some kind of super saints? No! Many of them had denied Christ just a short 50 days prior and experienced the most shattering disappointment of their lives as they watched Jesus die. But they remembered and repented. They wrestled and prevailed. They didn't give up with discouragement over their own weaknesses. They pressed in during the waiting. And when the fullness of time had come, they were right where they needed to be for God to do mighty things.

As we prepare for God to move in amazing ways in our region, don't give up too quickly. Let's press in and position ourselves rightly by dying to our sin nature, letting God mold us through the challenges we face and rest in utter dependence on Him through abiding and then watch what He will do. I can guarantee, you won't be disappointed!

Adena Hodges

About
the Author

Adena lives with her husband, Gil and their three teenagers in Antelope, CA. She and Gil are Intercessory Missionaries at the Rock House of Prayer. They also lead the ministry, *The Intercessor's Workshop,* training and equipping the body of Christ to advance God's kingdom through intercession. For more information on this ministry, go to: www.IntercessorsWorkshop.com

Adena also writes a weekly blog on prayer at www.1000waystopray.com.

Adena has also written *The Inheritance,* a novel about the journey of going from slavery to being the bride of Christ, a twist on the Snow White fairy tale. To order, go to www.BeyondHappilyEverAfter.org. Look for the next book in this series in 2014 called *The Great Awakening,* a story about revival based on Sleeping Beauty.

Adena Hodges